Pascal Siakam: The Inspiring Story of One of Basketball's Rising Stars

An Unauthorized Biography

By: Clayton Geoffreys

Table of Contents

Foreword

Every few years, a great underdog story is told in the basketball world. Jimmy Butler, Kawhi Leonard, Draymond Green, and Nikola Jokic are just a few examples of great recent non-lottery draft picks. Pascal Siakam's rise in the NBA has quickly become one of the latest impressive stories for finding high value players in the latter half of first round draft picks. Selected 27th overall in the 2016 NBA Draft, Siakam has quickly emerged as a rising star in the league. It's hard to believe that not too long ago, Siakam spent time in the NBA Development League as a member of the Toronto Raptors' affiliate team, the Raptors 905. Two seasons later, Siakam was a champion as a member of the 2019 Toronto Raptors. With Kawhi Leonard's departure from the Raptors in the 2019 offseason to return home, Siakam has a unique opportunity to take on a leading role for the franchise that drafted him. Thank you for purchasing *Pascal Siakam: The Inspiring Story of One of Basketball's*

Rising Stars. In this unauthorized biography, we will learn Pascal Siakam's incredible life story and impact on the game of basketball. Hope you enjoy and if you do, please do not forget to leave a review!

Also, check out my website at claytongeoffreys.com to join my exclusive list where I let you know about my latest books. To thank you for your purchase, you can go to my site to download a free copy of *33 Life Lessons: Success Principles, Career Advice & Habits of Successful People*. In the book, you'll learn from some of the greatest thought leaders of different industries on what it takes to become successful and how to live a great life.

Cheers,

Clayton Geoffreys

Visit me at www.claytongeoffreys.com

Introduction

The NBA is full of underdog stories that people all over the world love to follow. We have seen players that literally came from nowhere but suddenly became successful in the NBA and even went on to become stars or champions. These are the stories that are both heart-warming and sometimes tear-jerking because we cannot help but root for such players, who worked their hardest to get to the point where they could be successful in the NBA.

The league has never been short of such stories. LeBron James, who grew up without a father, only had his mother to rely on as he went on to use his physical gifts to become one of the greatest players in the world. Stephen Curry, who may have lived a comfortable life in his younger days, was considered someone who could not star in the NBA because of his lack of size and athleticism. However, he went on to become the only player in league history to win the MVP award unanimously.

If we are talking about players who lifted themselves from obscurity, we should never forget about Giannis Antetokounmpo. Called the "Greek Freak," Antetokounmpo used to peddle in the streets of his hometown in Greece but worked his way up to become an MVP-caliber player in the NBA. Then there is Joel Embiid, who was an unknown in Cameroon before he picked up basketball at the age of 15, but eventually became one of the greatest centers in the modern-day NBA.

Another Cameroonian had a story that is very similar to what Joel Embiid had gone through in life. Born in Cameroon, a developing country where basketball is still in its infancy stage, Pascal Siakam did not play basketball until he was about 15 years old. His life had a different direction during his early teen years, and he had little to no interest in becoming a basketball player much less an NBA player.

However, he was eventually discovered by a Cameroonian NBA player named Luc Mbah a Moute, who made it one of his goals to develop basketball in Cameroon and to search for players that have the talent to make it big in that sport. Mbah a Moute saw potential in Pascal Siakam because of his combination of size, mobility, and athleticism. It did not take long for Siakam to see himself going to the United States to try to improve in basketball in the hopes of becoming a professional.

Pascal Siakam initially struggled to find his place in the United States as he had to move from one camp to another. However, he was eventually recruited by New Mexico University, where he starred as a redshirt freshman after posting ridiculous numbers on both ends of the floor. He later declared for the NBA draft after two successful seasons in college.

However, even though Siakam was an effective player in New Mexico in the two years he spent there, he was not a highly-touted prospect in the 2016 NBA Draft. People raved about his athleticism and his mobility as a big man, but he was entering the draft as a raw prospect. Nobody thought of him as a star in the making, but he was still drafted by the Toronto Raptors with the 27th overall pick thinking he could be a part of their future as a versatile role player at the power forward position.

During his first two years in the league, Pascal Siakam did indeed look like he was going to be a capable role player. Despite winning the D-League (now G-League) Finals MVP and winning the D-League championship in his assignment as a member of the Rio Grande Valley Vipers during his rookie year in the NBA, he still looked like a raw player especially on the offensive end of the floor.

However, in his third season in the league, Pascal Siakam exploded from being a role player into a capable all-around threat for the Toronto Raptors. Using his athleticism and his supreme mobility, Siakam could turn himself into a matchup nightmare with a versatile offensive repertoire. On the defensive end, he could guard almost anyone out on the floor because of his mobility and strength. Siakam became the ultimate secondary player for the Raptors at that time and improved so much that he went on to become arguably the second-best player for Toronto at that time. Siakam went on to win the Most Improved Player that year.

Pascal Siakam's importance was highlighted during the 2019 NBA playoffs when the Raptors were able to make a deep run to the NBA Finals. He upped his scoring during the playoffs and was one of the main contributors for the Toronto Raptors on both ends of the floor. Then, in the Finals, it became clear that Siakam was a star on the making especially after showing how big of a matchup nightmare he was in Game 1. He had 32 points and shot 14 out of 17 from the floor in that game.

Throughout the Finals that year, Siakam stayed consistent and even put up a double-double in Game 6 when the Raptors defeated the Golden State Warriors to hoist their very first NBA championship. Pascal Siakam may have played a secondary role to Kawhi Leonard during the entire season up to the Finals, but everyone believed that the Toronto Raptors would not have gotten as far as they did had he did not make a massive jump from a role player into a guy that could become a star in the NBA.

After Kawhi Leonard left during the offseason of 2019, Pascal Siakam ultimately earned himself a more significant role. From the man that played second to Leonard, he went on to become the Toronto Raptors future as he was thrust into the limelight to fill in the massive gap left by the 2019 NBA Finals MVP. He was the bright spot of what was an otherwise successful offseason for the Toronto Raptors because the entire organization believed that he was on his way to becoming a star.

From being an overlooked player to becoming the NBA's Most Improved Player, Pascal Siakam now has a chance to prove that he could become the Raptors' franchise player. More importantly, he also has a chance to show the entire world how far working hard could get you. His is an underdog story that has already inspired many, especially after he won an NBA title. However, he continues to write that story and has the chance to make it one of the greatest journeys the league has ever seen.

Chapter 1: Childhood and Early Life

Pascal Siakam was born on April 2, 1994, in the city of Douala, which is the largest city in the entire country of Cameroon. He was born the youngest of four brothers to parents Tchamo and Victoire Siakam. Pascal was later raised in Bafia, Cameroon, where he went to school as a young boy. At the time when he was born, nobody even thought that Pascal had the makings of a good basketball player even though the family loved basketball.

Tchamo Siakam, Pascal's father, worked at a local transit company in one of the cities in Cameroon. Later on, in 2007, he went on to serve as the mayor of the small town of Makénéné, which has a tiny population of only about 16,000 people. While Tchamo was a dedicated public servant, he was more dedicated as a devout Catholic. He saw this very same dedication in his youngest son, Pascal.

At a young age, Tchamo saw how his son Pascal was so dedicated towards his faith that he was handpicked by the family to carry their Catholic ideals.[i] Pascal grew up in a basketball family that saw the three older Siakam boys developing their love for the sport at early ages. Basketball was not a common sport in Cameroon, but all of Pascal's brothers took the game up and eventually excelled at it. Even though the NBA or any other known basketball league was hardly broadcasted in Cameroon, the three older Siakam brothers were able to develop and hone their skills in that sport so much that they later on earned Division I scholarships in the United States. However, the youngest of the Siakam brothers had a different upbringing.

As a devout young Catholic, Pascal followed his family's wishes and had an early upbringing that was geared towards a life of faith. He was not interested in basketball and had probably never even seen an NBA game when he was a young boy. His only exposure to basketball at that early part of his life was through his brothers, who later on left Cameroon to seek greener pastures as college basketball players.

Growing up, Pascal wanted to be a soccer player. His dream was to be that of a professional soccer (or football in Africa) player because that was the biggest sport not only in Cameroon but in the entire African continent. He had the early makings of a good soccer player because of his size and mobility at his young age. However, he never came close to even pursuing that dream because he was sent to boarding school at the age of 11.[ii]

When Pascal turned 11, Tchamo Siakam sent his youngest son to the small town of Bafia, Cameroon, to go to school to St. Andrew's Seminary, a Catholic institution meant to train young boys to a life geared towards faith at an early age. The plan was simple: the Siakam family wanted Pascal to eventually live a life of faith and to become a priest to embody the family's commitment towards Catholicism.[i]

As dedicated a Catholic as Pascal Siakam was at that young age, he still wanted to dream for himself. Playing soccer professionally was his goal, but that dream was never going to materialize. Becoming a priest was not in his plans, but Pascal did not want to go against his father's wishes because of how much he respected the man to whom he looked up.[i] As such, the 11-year old Pascal packed his bags and went to Bafia, which is almost an eight-hour bus trip from the family's home in Douala.

Initially, Pascal never wanted to follow his father's wishes. It was a tradition in the family to go to school to a seminary as Tchamo believed that it helps forms a young man's values and academic fundamentals. Tchamo believed in the value of a good education and had previously sent all of Pascal's older brothers to the seminary to study.[iii]

Pascal Siakam already knew what the seminary had in store for him. His brothers had already told stories about how bad the food was and how strict the rules were. They had to do chores and wake up as early as 5:30 in the morning to do them. The worst of it all was that they were forced to live far away from home with no one to go to whenever they were sad and lonely. At 11 years old, Pascal was forced to live a life he never wanted in a small town called Bafia.

The town of Bafia is not the most recognizable places in the entire country of Cameroon. If you are not from Cameroon, there is a good chance that you might not have even heard of Bafia before. It is a simple town with a population of over 55,000 people. It actually is more like a village instead of a town. This was where Pascal was raised to become a Catholic priest.

In the town of Bafia, which is described to be less than prosperous, Pascal Siakam had to endure an early part of his life he did not exactly plan. Bafia has all the problems one would expect from an impoverished town. People were suffering from diseases, drought, and the lack of a proper hospital or clinic in the area. The worst part was that they did not have access to a potable water supply. The only way they could get clean water was through a single property where an opulent home stood. Sometimes, the owner of the property allowed the villagers to collect clean water from the well there.[i] Siakam was one of the few young children who had to endure such a task of going to that home so he could gain access to potable water.

Raised to be a priest in St. Andrew's Seminary, Pascal Siakam lived a less than respectable life that saw him staying at a cramped institution. He and many other boys were tasked to do chores early in the morning. Such duties were not entirely difficult. However, under the heat of the African sun and in an institution that was not the most suitable place to live, such chores were not the ideal things a young boy should be doing at the age of 11. Yet, Pascal did so impressively when he was young.

Living in the seminary meant that Pascal Siakam had to follow the institution's schedule to the letter. He had to do his chores early in the morning before attending to his academic duties. Pascal was described as a punctual young boy who did his responsibilities with enthusiasm. He was always punctual with his work and was also one of the more excellent young boys in St. Andrew's.

However, as the years went on, Pascal's behavior suddenly changed. Instead of the dutiful and responsible young boy that the Catholic priests enjoyed seeing, the young Siakam suddenly lost his enthusiasm. He gradually began to slack off when it came to his chores and his academic responsibilities. The young boy who used to be the top student in his class began to lose his interest in his studies. He stopped doing his homework, and his grades started to slide.

St. Andrew's Seminary had strict rules that the students had to follow. There were days when the boys were allowed to leave the property to go wherever they needed to. However, Pascal became rebellious and acted out on his own. He went on to leave the seminary grounds whenever he wanted to and only came back whenever it pleased him. Pascal became a stubborn young boy to the disappointment of the priests running the institution.

There were times when the priests were very close to wanting to dismiss Pascal Siakam from the seminary and to send him back to his parents to Douala. However, they thought that Pascal was too smart of a young boy to let go. They allowed the teenager to stay even though they were so close to giving up on him and the possibility of him becoming a good Catholic priest.

However, it was never Pascal Siakam's fault for acting out. After all, he originally never wanted to be there personally and was only in the seminary to try to please his father's wish of him becoming a Catholic priest. The young Pascal was even crying as much as he could when he first got to St. Andrew's. At times, he called his sister Vanessa, who was living in South Africa at that time, trying to remind himself that he had someone who could talk to whenever he was sad.

Time passed, and Pascal Siakam's behavior and outlook hardly changed. He went on with his regular schedule of activities and tried his best to do his responsibilities. At that time, his brothers were in the United States trying to develop as basketball players in the hopes of earning themselves a good future in the sport. However, Pascal was nowhere near the basketball player he is right now at that point in his life.

The boys of St. Andrew's Seminary had one hour a day for any physical activity of their choosing. Still sad about not being able to fulfill his dreams of becoming a professional soccer player, Pascal Siakam spent that one hour per day playing the sport all by himself. At times, he changed his approach a bit and shot a basketball at the property's makeshift basketball rim, which was not in the best shape to help develop a young teenager's skill at that sport. Those rare occasions were the only times Pascal was exposed to the sport. Other than that, he never had any formal training in basketball. Siakam did not see himself actually becoming a basketball player. Of course, in the first place, he never wanted to become one.

Before he went to Bafia, playing soccer was his dream. He knew he had the makings of a good basketball player, but he wanted to do something original because all three of his older brothers were already playing basketball. As such, one of his biggest dreams was to make it to a professional soccer team. The seminary prevented him from such fulfilling that dream. However, Pascal also had backup plans. He wanted to become a successful businessman or to serve in the government alongside his father, who was already a town mayor at that time.[iii] Staying in St. Andrew's made him unsure of what he wanted but what Pascal was sure of at that time was that he wanted to be anywhere else but in Bafia.

At the age of 15, Siakam had already admitted to himself that he did not want to become a priest and that he did not like the life he lived in St. Andrew's Seminary. The young teenager thought that misbehaving and doing whatever he wanted to do was enough for the priests to dismiss him and to send him back to his parents. Whatever the priests were doing was not working. They tried to discipline the young Siakam, but Pascal only lashed out even more. It was a relationship that was not working anymore.[i] It became too tedious and tiresome to both parties that they hardly got anything good from such a setup anymore.

Eventually, the priests running St. Andrew's Seminary decided to send Pascal Siakam back to Douala temporarily hoping that he could sort things out with his family and find a renewed passion once he returned to Bafia. Tchamo also wanted Pascal to fulfill his obligations by going back to Bafia after getting a much-needed break in Douala.

Father Collins, the priest in charge of St. Andrew's Seminary, understood as much that Pascal Siakam did not share in his father's vision. That was what led Pascal, who was described as a smart and hardworking kid, to suddenly start doing dumb and stupid things to get himself in trouble. Collins also understood that it was already a foregone conclusion that they were not going to make Pascal into a priest. However, the least they were hoping to do was to help turn him into a more disciplined young man.

In 2012, Pascal Siakam graduated from the institution and went on to pack his bags for good. He went on to leave Bafia, knowing for himself that becoming a priest was not the right path for him. At that point, he and even Father Collins knew that the biggest problem that Pascal had was that he did not know what to do. He had all the talent and the brains to excel at whatever to which he put his mind. Yet, the problem was that he did not know where to put all that effort.

Living in Bafia might not have been the best part of Pascal Siakam's life, but his stay there did leave a lasting impression. That one good house that stood out in such a small town that lived in poverty was what gave Siakam the hope he needed. The house was proof that he could also become a successful person in his own right. Who owned that house? NBA player Luc Mbah a Moute's parents.[i]

Chapter 2: Learning How to Play Basketball

Before graduating from St. Andrew's Seminary and in the middle of a summer break in 2011, Pascal Siakam had a chance to change his life by attending a basketball camp started by Luc Mbah a Moute in the hopes of finding raw talent in the country of Cameroon and to encourage young men to pick up basketball so that it might grow to become just as popular as soccer is.

Luc Mbah a Moute, at that time, was the poster boy of basketball in the country of Cameroon. There have not been many Cameroonian NBA players. After all, basketball is not a big sport in Cameroon or anywhere else in Africa, for that matter. However, Mbah a Moute was one of the few players who made a long journey from Cameroon to the United States in the hopes of fulfilling a basketball dream. After staying a few seasons in UCLA, Mbah a Moute was drafted into the NBA in 2008 to become only the second player born and raised in Cameroon to make it to the big leagues

While Mbah a Moute was never close to becoming a star in the NBA, he defined his career as a great role player who used his strength, mobility, motor, and athleticism to his advantage especially on the defensive end. He became a respectable defensive stopper that was tasked to defend superstar forwards such as LeBron James, Kevin Durant, and Kawhi Leonard. He never stayed too long in one team but was always someone that teams looked to pick up as a free agent because of his defensive versatility and his ability to act as a glue guy for his team in the locker room.

When Mbah a Moute started his quest to look for great basketball talents in Cameroon, he was still a member of the Milwaukee Bucks and was one of their best role players. It was during his stay with the Bucks that he discovered future NBA star Joel Embiid, who is just about two weeks older than Siakam. Embiid picked up basketball when he was 15 years old, which means that he could learn how to play the sport about two years ahead of Pascal. Joel Embiid eventually moved to the United States to finish his high school studies there and to play college basketball.

In 2011, Pascal Siakam tagged along with his friends to join one of Mbah a Moute's free basketball camps. Because he was carrying his older brothers' names, his reputation as a Siakam earned him a chance to participate in Mbah a Moute's basketball camp. However, neither he nor the people behind that camp had several expectations. After all, he was supposed to be the least likely to become a good basketball player out of all four brothers.

However, what Siakam had that his brothers did not was a profound untapped potential just waiting for the right time to materialize. At that time, Pascal Siakam had many things in common with Joel Embiid. He might have been skinny, raw, and unpolished as far as basketball skills were concerned. However, he was far more athletic and mobile than any other young man in that camp. Best of all, he was competitive enough to play against any physicality thrown at him.[i] He did not look like much of a basketball player at that time, but his body language, motor, and effort levels showed how much untapped potential he had in the skinny frame of a teenager who was once supposed to be a priest.

After graduating from St. Andrew's in 2012, Pascal Siakam made a decision that changed the course of his career. A young man that previously did not have a direction in life because he did not know what he wanted to do, Siakam returned to Luc Mbah a Moute's camp in 2012 to further hone his basketball skills. At that time, Siakam had a faint idea of what he wanted to do in his life. He gave basketball a shot and was willing to learn the sport in the hopes of making it his ticket to a finer life. True to what Father Collins said about him, Pascal worked his tail off because he already knew what he wanted to do in his life.

During the camp, Pascal Siakam was chosen to take part in the African edition of Basketball Without Borders, which is an instructional camp organized by the NBA in partnership with FIBA as a way of helping young people all around the world develop their skills in basketball and their love and appreciation for the sport. As one of the few young men chosen to take part in such a prestigious camp, Pascal Siakam knew that doing well there could earn him a shot at a life in America as a basketball player.

Pascal Siakam entered the basketball camp not knowing what it was all about or who the people there were. The 6'9" young man even asked why people were flocking over towards two large men. When he was told that those two men were Luol Deng and Serge Ibaka, who themselves became outstanding

NBA players, Siakam did not even know who they were even though they were known all over Africa as two of the greatest African players in the NBA at that time.[ii]

It was understandable. Pascal Siakam did not know a thing about basketball or the NBA at that time aside from the things heard from his older brothers. He only attended Luc Mbah a Moute's basketball camp a year ago for the fun of it. In 2012, he only attended the Basketball Without Borders camp because he wanted to find a way to America hoping he could get a college scholarship like his brothers.

Siakam went on to learn more about Deng and Ibaka, the latter of which later became his teammate in the NBA. By learning more about those two African NBA players, Pascal Siakam also learned how tough it was to get to the NBA. Suddenly, learning basketball for fun and for the possibility of making it to the US turned into a dream for Siakam. His new goal was not to merely go to America to play college basketball but to ultimately become an NBA player.

At that time, Masai Ujiri, who was working as the general manager of the Denver Nuggets was a witness to Pascal Siakam's raw talent. Ujiri himself was once an NBA player who had a career that did not last long. However, this English-born Nigerian made waves not as a basketball player but as a team executive who knew how to assess talent and build a competitive team around players with talent and potential. Masai Ujiri, who once won the NBA's Executive of the Year award and later moved on to become the president of basketball operations of the Toronto Raptors, closely followed the growth of basketball in the continent of Africa.

During the 2012 Basketball Without Borders, Masai Ujiri was there to observe the growing pool of talented players in Africa. He saw a 17-year old Pascal Siakam, who knew what was at stake there and was playing better than he ever had to in the past in the hopes of impressing the scouts that observed them. Ujiri was one of the many people impressed by Siakam's abilities. However, what impressed the future Raptors executive was not Siakam's talents and skills but his raw physical attributes. At his height, he could move with the fluidity of a guard and the athleticism of a forward. However, what made him stand out was his effort. Siakam's activity and motor out on the floor made him the main attraction of that year's African leg of Basketball Without Borders.

Flying out of nowhere to block shots, diving for loose balls to get an extra possession, moving quickly into position to grab an offensive rebound, and dunking the ball hard using his athletic legs, Siakam had a commendable performance in that basketball camp. His skills were still raw, and he could barely shoot the ball, but Masai Ujiri loved his effort. However, as Ujiri himself admitted, Pascal Siakam did not look like an NBA player back then.[i]

Nevertheless, whatever Pascal Siakam displayed in the Basketball Without Borders camp was already enough for him to catch the attention of scouts. He was not outstanding in the camp, and he did not showcase the same set of skills that some of the other campers possessed. In short, he was one of the many young men who had unrefined basketball skills. However, his motor and raw physical abilities were what caught the attention of one scout.

A scout from God's Academy, a prep school in Lewisville, Texas, approached the young Pascal Siakam and offered him a chance to go to the United States. Not knowing a bit of English, Pascal Siakam was hesitant at first even though he originally wanted to go to America for a chance to become an NBA player. After all, it was going to be an entirely new journey for him. Moving to Bafia at the age of 11 was already a great adjustment for him. Going to the United States thousands of miles away from home was a different story.

However, Tchamo Siakam, who originally wanted his youngest son to become a Catholic priest, encouraged Pascal to take the chance to go to the United States. Tchamo wanted one his sons to make it to the NBA. This was Pascal's chance to fulfill his father's dream after failing to give in to Tchamo's wishes of him becoming a priest. Pascal wanted to make his father proud of him this time. He was not merely working hard for his own dream but also for his father's wishes.[ii]

James Siakam, Pascal's brother, was playing for Vanderbilt as a 6'7" forward at that time. James was entering his sophomore year when Pascal called him to tell him of the good news. However, James could not believe it at first. He thought that his youngest brother was joking around because he never thought that Pascal was interested in basketball.[i] For James, it was odd for Pascal and the word "basketball" to be in the same sentence.

Christian Siakam, who played for IUPUI at that time, thought that it was also a joke that Pascal was going to the United States to play basketball. The last time Christian heard anything about his younger brother was that he was shorter than he was and that he was studying to become a priest. However, when the Siakam parents called him to tell him of the good news and to tell him that Pascal had grown taller than he was, he laughed hard because he knew that Pascal and basketball did not go together.[iv]However, both he and James eventually believed it. Pascal was heading to the United States for a chance to become a basketball player.

When Pascal moved to God's Academy, he began to realize how much of a struggle it was to fulfill his new dream of becoming an NBA player. The North American culture was entirely different from the one he was accustomed to in Cameroon. He struggled with communicating with people because he hardly spoke English. He also realized that the basketball in the

United States was a different monster compared to the African brand of basketball that he played back home.

Back in Africa, Pascal Siakam excelled because he was taller and more athletic than all the other players with whom he played. He could dominate basketball using his effort and his athletic abilities. After all, those tools were what ultimately got him the chance to move to the United States. However, the reality was that such tools were not going to make him one of the best players in America.

The Americans that Siakam had to compete with were just as tall and just as athletic as him. More importantly, they had years of training and experience under their belts already. The teenagers that he played against had much more refined basketball skills and were seemingly better built than he was for that sport. There were even times when his teammates mocked him because of how raw of a player he was and how he struggled to speak English.[ii]

He heard every bit of insult his teammates threw at him. Whenever he tried to handle the ball, his teammates told him to give up trying because he did not have such a gift. Whenever his jumpers were nowhere near making it through the basket, the other players laughed at him for bricking his shots.[iii] It seemed as if he could not do anything right and that he had to start from scratch all over again.

However, what Pascal Siakam possessed that not many American players did not was his innate drive to do what it took to become better and to make an impact. He was always willing to chase after loose balls and to jump up against bigger and stronger players for rebounds. His motor was something that no one else had. It was like he was fighting for his life every time he was on the court. It was this innate ability that ultimately got him a chance to play college basketball.

Pascal Siakam did not get many college offers from big-name programs. However, New Mexico was interested in the young Cameroonian precisely because of his innate motor. Former New Mexico head coach Marvin Menzies said that he thought that Pascal did not have a good set of basketball skills. However, what got him to love the young Siakam was his motor.[iii] Skills can be taught, but a player's motor and desire to put a hundred percent into everything is a trait that can never be coached. Long story short, Pascal Siakam was one step closer to his NBA dream when he decided to go to New Mexico to pursue a college basketball career.

Chapter 3: College Career

Freshman Year

One year after leaving Cameroon to play basketball in the United States, Pascal Siakam was adjusting to the new life he had to live. Moving to New Mexico was a new challenge for him. He had to learn how to become a responsible adult living in America. The freshman was learning how to pay his bills, know where and what to eat, and speak English. It was a difficult period of adjustment for Pascal Siakam. Had he not been a stronger person, he would have packed his bags and went straight back to Cameroon, where he would have been able to live a modest but easier life.

Pascal Siakam's freshman year with the New Mexico Aggies did not start as well as he had hoped. The 18-year old freshman, who had just learned how to play basketball about two years ago, struggled to adjust to the level of his peers in college basketball. If he thought that playing high school basketball just a year after performing well in Cameroon was tough, college was very different.

In his own words, Pascal Siakam got his butt kicked every day while he was trying to learn how to play college basketball. His teammates were a lot better than he was and were better equipped to handle the rigors and grinds of college basketball. Siakam lacked the skill and the experience to play well with his teammates. Siakam did not kid when he said that he got his butt handed to him every time he was practicing with the team. The man kicking him in practices was a South African native named Tshilidzi Nephawe.

Nephawe was not only older than Siakam but was a lot bigger and stronger. He was a 6'10" hulk of a young man who weighed about 270 pounds. Meanwhile, Siakam had just grown to about 6'9" and was barely 200 pounds of skin and bones. Every time Nephawe had him on defense, Siakam got beaten up physically.

On the other end of the floor, he could not do anything on Nephawe.[iii] This was what made Pascal realize that he needed to do plenty of work on the physical aspect of the game because college players were bigger and stronger than the ones he faced in high school.

Unfortunately for Pascal Siakam, he was forced to redshirt his first year as a college basketball player because of academic issues. After all, he was still in the middle of a significant adjustment period both in terms of living as a college basketball player and as a college student. However, Siakam did not waste that one season he had to miss. Throughout that year, he did all that he could to become a better basketball player equipped with the proper tools, skills, and knowledge.

When Siakam was out of the lineup, he was not only determined to work hard on his game but also on his knowledge about basketball and his English-speaking skills as well. He turned to Paul Weir, an assistant in

New Mexico, for help. Weir allowed him to hit two birds with one stone by giving him different types of basketball books, which included the legendary Dean Smith's *Basketball*.[iii] The purpose was to help him learn how to speak English while giving him an avenue to learn more about basketball off the court.

To his surprise, Weir saw Siakam more often than expected because the young man was asking him for more books. Pascal Siakam had soaked up all the knowledge in those books quicker than most other people and was hungry to learn more. He was trying to learn how to become a better basketball player and to learn more about the new country in which he was living. Weir thought that Siakam was more mature and focused than any of his other peers simply because of the kind of dedication he was displaying at his age.

On the court, Pascal Siakam was also putting in the necessary work to become a better player. Whenever he was free, he spent his time in the gym honing his skills, learning how to shoot, dribble, and pass the ball like he was a middle school player trying to learn how to play basketball for the first time in his life. All this was because of his father.

Whenever he had a chance to do so, Pascal Siakam called back home to give his family updates about his life in the United States and how far he has gone ever since learning how to play basketball for the first time when in 2011. While talking to his father, he could feel how proud he was of him. Pascal's past transgressions and failures when he was still in St. Andrew's Seminary were too heavy for his conscience to carry, and he believed that his father was still upset about him not pursuing the path of a Catholic priest. However, with his ongoing success in America, Pascal also realized that his father had already learned to forgive him. That said, making his father even more proud was what fueled Pascal Siakam to work harder than he ever did.

Pascal Siakam spent plenty of time in the weight room for the first time in his life. From the skinny Cameroonian kid, who was barely 200 pounds of skin and bones, he grew into a lean athlete by adding about 30 pounds of muscle. He lifted weights, ate right, and focused on making sure that whatever weight he gained was pure muscle so that he could stay mobile and active on the court.[iv]

That was not all because Siakam seemingly had to learn from scratch. All that he got going for him at that point was his effort and his drive. His coaches had to show him different video clips he could study and use as an example. To their surprise, he was like a sponge that quickly absorbed everything he saw and applied it on the court just as effectively as they would have wanted. They thought that Siakam was not merely an active and driven player but was also a smart and brilliant young man who was quick to learn new things.

In 2014, after an entire year of working on his game, Pascal Siakam saw Nephawe again and matched up with him. While he still had a long way to go before being big and strong enough to beat the South African, he more than held his ground against the bigger player. This was when he thought that he was already physically ready to take the grind of a college basketball season.

However, things turned for the worse for Pascal Siakam. In October of 2014, he learned from his sister Raissa, who was living in Washington at that time, that his father had passed away. Days before the call, Tchamo was in a car accident that sent him to the hospital. It took a few days for him to succumb to the internal injuries he sustained from the car crash. However, up to now, the details are still unclear for Pascal and his brothers because they did not have to heart to ask their sobbing mother what had transpired from the car crash up to the point of Tchamo's death.[i] All they knew at that time was that their father had passed away before seeing one of his sons making it to the NBA.

At that point, everything else was a blank for Pascal Siakam. The one thing he wanted to do was to go home. He wanted to forget about being in college, about basketball, and about making it to the NBA. All he wanted to do was to go back to Cameroon to see his father for the last time and to comfort his mother in her time of grief. However, it was Victoire herself who pleaded Pascal not to go home.

Victoire Siakam, as sad as she was at the time of her husband's death, still thought that what Pascal needed to do at that time was what Tchamo would have wanted him to do. She prevented her son from coming home because he knew that her husband would have wanted Pascal to stay in the US to pursue the NBA dream.

Pascal realized what he needed to do. He stayed in the United States to pursue a dream his father would have wanted him to reach. His goal was no longer to make the NBA so he could have a house as nice as the one that Luc Mbah a Moute's parents have in Bafia. It also was no longer to be able to get back on Nephawe for kicking his butt so hard in practice. It was to make his father proud of him. Pascal Siakam felt unstoppable because he was playing not for himself but the late Tchamo Siakam.[iii]

Head coach Marvin Menzies was there to comfort his player because he knew how hard it was to lose a father. However, Menzies also told Siakam that he needed to stay in the US because he risked losing his chance to make it to the NBA if he had gone home to Cameroon for his father's funeral. To that end, Siakam already knew what he needed to do and dedicated the upcoming season to his father.[i]

Due to several reasons, Pascal Siakam was not even supposed to play during the 2014-15 season, but he eventually made it to the lineup as a redshirt freshman.

In his first college basketball game, he had seven points in only about 20 minutes in a loss to Wichita State. However, he began learning how to play better quicker than anyone would have expected. In just his third game of the season, he went for 19 points and five blocks in the Aggies' win over Northern Colorado. Then, on November 24, 2014, against Stetson, he performed in a way that embodied his personality. He fought for every possession as if his life depended on it. In turn, he ended up with 12 offensive rebounds for a total of 17 boards in a win for New Mexico.

Siakam's amazing play at the start of the season, as well as an injury to Nephawe, prompted the coaching staff to give Pascal Siakam the starting nod. Barely four years since he started playing basketball back in 2011, Pascal Siakam was already better than most of his teammates. He was putting up double-digit scoring performances at an efficient rate while also pulling down rebounds at a high clip because of his motor and relentless activity. Siakam was all heart and hustle and was playing with a purpose none of the other players on the court could understand.

On December 27, Pascal Siakam had a double-double performance of 13 points and 13 rebounds in a loss to Colorado State. A game after that, he went for a new career-high of 21 points after making nine of his 14 shots from the field in a win over Texas Southern. It took a while for Siakam to break that career-high in scoring. It was on February 12, 2015, when he went for 24 points after making eight of his 11 shots in a win over Seattle. Pascal Siakam ended his freshman year losing to Kansas in the opening round of the NCAA Tournament.

Ever since scoring 19 points in his first game that season, Siakam went on to score in double digits 22 times in the next 27 games. He was a consistent threat for New Mexico, who relied on his ability to clean the glass and go for hustle points. As terrific of a contributor as he was, Pascal Siakam was not their main option on offense and was just someone who got by using his motor and hustle to get into a good scoring position.

In his freshman year for New Mexico, Pascal Siakam averaged 12.8 points, 7.7 rebounds, and 1.8 blocks. He shot 57.2% from the floor and had grown so much that he was the team's second-leading scorer. He even finished that season with stats better than Tshilidzi Nephawe, who used to eat him up alive when they were matched up together during practices. Because of Siakam's terrific play that season, he was awarded the Western Athletic Conference Freshman of the Year.

After his redshirt freshman season, Pascal Siakam seriously did not think that he was ready to make the jump to the NBA. He also did not think about his dream of becoming an NBA player. All that he ever thought of at that point was to continue to get better hoping that he could someday be good enough to get to have a shot at the NBA. That was what he did in his sophomore season with New Mexico.

Sophomore Year

New Mexico's top scoring options had played out their final year of eligibility. Meanwhile, Pascal Siakam had finished out a breakout season that surprised plenty of people because nobody thought that this Cameroonian, who had been in the United States for three years, was already quickly becoming one of the best college players in the country.

Siakam's sophomore year was one that saw him becoming his team's best player and their top option on both offense and defense. In just his first game that season, he already exceeded expectations by going for a new career-high of 26 points to go along with ten rebounds in a win over Houston Baptist on November 13, 2015. Then, five days later, he broke that mark by going for 30 points, 11 rebounds, and four assists in a win over Tennessee Tech.

Against the Air Force team on November 28, Pascal Siakam had an amazing all-around effort by going for 26 points, 12 rebounds, and six blocks. In the very next game, which was against UTEP, he had an even better output. In that win for New Mexico, Siakam finished with 24 points, 23 rebounds, and five blocks. At that point, he had already solidified himself as a premier double-double threat that could score, rebound, and block shots at a high rate.

Pascal Siakam went on to tie his career-high in points on December 21 in a win over Oral Roberts. The Cameroonian finished that game with 35 points on 13 out of 21 shooting from the field while also collecting 11 points. At that point of the season, Siakam was looking more like a beast. In his first 12 games, he had ten double-doubles and scored 20 or more points eight times.

Defenses began to adjust to Siakam's surprising play as no one knew how good he was going to turn out to be at the early part of the season. While his scoring may have dropped a bit, teams had no way of stopping his motor and his effort. He continued to rebound the ball at a terrific rate while also making an impact on the defensive end as a great shot-blocker. Pascal Siakam even finished with a career-high of seven blocks in a win over Cal State Bakersfield on February 18, 2016. He may have finished that game shooting one out of 12 but he more than made up for a poor shooting performance with his defense. That was always the kind of player Siakam has been. He may struggle as a scorer at times, but he will never forget to play defense and to hustle for rebounds and defensive plays.

Pascal Siakam and New Mexico failed to do some damage that season. They could not qualify for the NCAA Tournament and even failed to take the conference title. However, things were not so bad on the part of Siakam has he was named the WAC Player of the Year after averaging amazing numbers of 20.3 points, 11.6 rebounds, and 2.2 blocks. On top of that, he did not force his shots and was not the best player on the team by default considering that he was shooting 54% from the floor and making an impact on both ends of the court.

After getting named his conference's most outstanding player, Pascal Siakam was ready to contemplate on whether or not he was ready for the NBA. He may have posted great numbers in his sophomore year, but there were many things to consider aside from stats. Nevertheless, the NBA had become a possibility for him just five years after he started learning how to play basketball.

Pascal Siakam was ready to take the biggest plunge of his life. From a boy who was halfheartedly studying to become a priest, he picked up basketball at the age of 16 and only dreamed of becoming an NBA player at such a late age. Now, he was well on his way to making his dreams come true as he had a good chance of getting drafted after two years of playing college basketball for New Mexico.

Chapter 4: NBA Career

Getting Drafted

Pascal Siakam, at first, was not sure whether or not he could already go pro with the skills he was bringing to the table. However, he was lucky enough that there was a new rule for college basketball players saying that they could withdraw their names from the NBA draft ten days after the scouting combine. What that meant for Siakam was that he could assess whether or not there were teams who were willing to give him a shot at a roster spot.

At first, Pascal Siakam worked out with several teams. However, what stood out was the workout he had with the Toronto Raptors. At that time, he was set to work out on the same day with lottery prospects Jakob Poeltl and Skal Labissiere. Both of those players are bigger and were also rated higher than Siakam. Because of that, Siakam psyched himself up, thinking that he would work out alongside Poeltl and Labissiere. He was thinking of dunking hard on their heads and of sending their shots flying over to the stands.[iii]

However, Siakam did not get a chance to play against those two seven-footers because they were given solo workouts. Nonetheless, he already had enough pent-up energy in him that he could excel in his workout with the Toronto Raptors. At first, he did not think that the Raptors were interested in him. After all, he was not one of the top-rated prospects of that year's draft class.

He thought that other teams were not very interested in him as well. He got mixed responses from the teams for which he worked out. Some said that he was going to be taken late in the first round while others thought he was going to be taken in the second round. There were those who said that he should take his talents to Europe before trying to make a career in the NBA.

Siakam himself contemplated on returning for one more year in New Mexico to further hone his skills.

However, Pascal Siakam took a deep plunge. When the deadline for withdrawing passed, Siakam remained a prospect hoping to get drafted that year. It was one of the biggest gambles he took in his life because he did not even know whether or not he was going to get drafted. Yet, as good as Siakam was in his second year in New Mexico, why exactly was he not one of the top prospects? Let us first examine Pascal Siakam's profile as an NBA prospect.

Physically, there were no problems with Siakam's tools. Standing at 6'9" and weighing 230 pounds, he was coming into the NBA with the right height and body build for the power forward position. Moreover, he has a wingspan of about 7'3", which came in handy on defense and when going up against bigger and taller defenders.

Pascal Siakam is also an athletically gifted player. He may be a big man, but he never moved much like someone standing 6'9". The Cameroonian already had the fluidity and quickness of a smaller forward. He could also move with the grace of a guard. His mobility was always his best asset. On top of that, he is an excellent athlete that could quickly jump higher than most other players standing 6'9" or taller.

Offensively, Siakam is as terrific a finisher as one could find. He made more than 62% of his shots near the basket in his final year in New Mexico. Most of the shots he converted were off passes from teammates whenever he is cutting to the basket or off offensive rebounds after finding a good position for himself after a missed shot. Using his length, he can finish well for a man who does not have the biggest frame or the most explosive leaping ability.[v]

Pascal Siakam also proved himself a capable player in transition. He is much faster and much more mobile than most other big men that he could easily outrun them on the break. As such, he scored several his points in transition as a finisher by being the first player down the court after one of his teammates rebounded the ball.

On the defensive end, Pascal Siakam has shown himself as a capable defender. In a day and age where switching has become a crucial defensive strategy for most teams to prevent guards from getting the space and look they need from the three-point area, Siakam is a player that fits the bill of what a switch-heavy team needs from a big man.

Because of his mobility, lateral quickness, and length, scouts thought that Siakam had what it took to become an effective defender in the NBA. Using his long arms and his leaping ability, he can protect the basket. When switched out on guards, he as the mobility and the length to make life difficult for perimeter players. That said, he already had the makings of a good defender both out on the perimeter and down at the low post. Think of a lankier but taller version of Draymond Green.

As a rebounder, there were also reasons to believe the Pascal Siakam was going to be an effective player at rebounding the basketball in the NBA. Many of his rebounds were coming off his effort and hustle instead of knowing how to position himself or using his body to box other rebounders out. Nevertheless, he was set to be a more than capable rebounder in the NBA give his mobility, effort level, and length.

However, what was deemed Pascal Siakam's best asset was his motor. One would be hard-pressed to find a player with the same drive and motor that Siakam has on the floor. He is always the first one running down the court in transition. He always fights for rebounds and loose balls. He never forgets to hustle for a weakside block or to make things difficult for the shooter. It was this kind of a motor and effort on both ends of the floor that was innate in Siakam. While there were other players with skills that were much more refined, no coach could ever teach Siakam's drive to put in a hundred percent of his effort in every single play. He plays every single minute as if his life depended on it.[vi]

However, there was only so much effort and hustle can do for you in the NBA. You can make it to the big leagues by being a great effort player, but you certainly will not become a star if you merely rely on your motor without honing your skills. Pascal Siakam was one of the players scouts believed was not ready to make a big impact in the NBA as far as his skills were concerned.

In college, Siakam was all heart, hustle, and effort but did not showcase too much skill. He did not show himself to be a good scorer when he has the ball down in the low post. Instead, most of his shots came off his teammates' shot-creation and his ability to position himself for open shots near the basket or offensive rebounds. His ability to play in transition as a finisher also came in handy. However, when given the ball in his hands, he struggled to create his own shot.

Siakam was not a player you could simply give the ball to and hope that he could create offense. He did not have a consistent jump shot (though his shot did not have bad mechanics). He also struggled to handle the ball at times and was not an effective player at driving to the basket with the ball in his hands.

Knowing how to finish strong off a drive was also a problem for Siakam. In the few occasions that he drives to the rim, he does not get to the basket. As such, he usually relied on floaters or off-balanced jumpers instead of going for strong layups or dunks at the rim. What that meant was that, at that point in his career, he was not going to be a reliable pick-and-roll player if he does not get to the basket to finish plays strong.

On the defensive end, while Pascal Siakam did indeed show flashes of his versatility as a defender, the sample size was far too small to assess what he could do as a defender in the NBA. New Mexico played zone defense, which allowed Siakam to play more as a help defender rather than as a primary one-on-one defender. As such, he was not able to play much one-on-one defense either at the post or out on the perimeter.[v] There were still questions of whether or not he could effectively stop an offensive play as a primary defender instead of as a help defender.

Some other intangibles also turned teams off. The first thing to look at was that Siakam was already 22 years old heading into the NBA draft because he had to spend three years and two seasons in college to develop into the player he was at that point in his career. At that time, NBA teams valued younger players because they had more room to grow as compared to the older ones. In a sense, teams thought that Siakam did not have a lot more room to grow because of his comparatively advanced age.

Another intangible that teams looked at was Siakam's experience. Most players vying for a spot in the NBA already had more than a decade of experience of playing organized basketball. However, Siakam only started learning how to play the game in 2011. It was only in 2012 when he started to approach it seriously. The same year, he played his first brand of organized basketball in his lone prep season. In the three years he spent in college, he was only able to play organized basketball for two seasons. That meant that, in the five years that have passed since Siakam learned how to play the sport, he only had three years of playing organized basketball.

Regardless of how smart he is and how quick he is to pick up instructions, experience always comes into play especially in the toughest moments of a game. Experience is what plenty of players rely on in tough situations because they have been through similar situations in the past. Pascal Siakam was not someone who could say the same because he picked up basketball in the second half of his teen years.

On the night of the 2016 NBA Draft, Pascal Siakam saw familiar names getting picked ahead of him. However, he was not even in New York for the draft because he opted to stay in Orlando after a workout with the Magic. As such, he watched the entire event from a television alongside his family and friends. They were all nervous as the first round was nearing its end.

Then, for the 27th pick of the draft, NBA Commissioner Adam Silver announced that the Toronto Raptors were taking Pascal Siakam. The moment he heard his name from the television, Siakam lost it. He did not have any words to describe what he was feeling at that point. All he did was cry. His brothers and his friends were all crying as well. The youngest Siakam, who was supposed to be a priest, was now an NBA player. He fulfilled his father's wishes through sheer hard work and determination.

The only thing that Pascal would have hoped for was that Tchamo was there to see him fulfilling the family's dreams. Seeing how his father would have reacted was his biggest wish at that time. However, as he and his brothers were all there huddling and hugging each other, they were all thinking about their father. They had helped to make what was once an impossible dream into a reality. Siakam made it to the NBA.

In the years that have passed since the 2016 NBA Draft, only top overall pick Ben Simmons has made it to an NBA All-Star Game. If you look at the other players that were chosen ahead of Pascal Siakam, you could make an argument that he has now grown to be better than most of them. Had teams known that Siakam's drive and hard work helped develop him into the star he is right now, they would have probably taken him just after Simmons that year.

Nevertheless, Pascal Siakam was drafted at the right time by the right team. The Raptors were the perfect team for him. However, more importantly, he was on his way to the NBA regardless of who took him and how long he had to wait for his name to get called. After all, the dream was to make it to the NBA after he had made so many sacrifices and taken so many risks. Tchamo would have truly been proud of his youngest son.

Rookie Season, G-League Finals MVP

When Pascal Siakam joined the Toronto Raptors, he was set to become a part of a team that was already a perennial playoff contender. Led by All-Star guards DeMar DeRozan and Kyle Lowry, the Raptors were in the middle of arguably the franchise's most successful era even though they were still unable to make it to the NBA Finals. That team was always going to win at least 50 games in a season. It was built to become one of the better squads in the Eastern Conference.

Pascal Siakam found himself in a good spot when he signed his rookie contract. The Toronto Raptors did not have a starting power forward despite how deep that team is. As such, Siakam got the nod from head coach Dwane Casey to become the team's starting power forward while the team's other power forward, the veteran Patrick Patterson, played off the bench where he was most effective.

On October 26, 2016, Pascal Siakam made his NBA debut in an official regular-season NBA game. He started that game for the Toronto Raptors and played 22 minutes in a win over the Detroit Pistons. He was a deciding factor for the team as his energy and hustle allowed him to make a difference. Siakam finished with four points and nine rebounds in his first-ever NBA game. Coincidentally, that game was also the first NBA game he has ever seen live and in person.

Continuing to become a difference-maker at the starting power forward spot because of his energy and defensive versatility, Siakam had his first double-digit scoring game on November 6. In that loss to the Sacramento Kings, he had ten points and six rebounds. In a loss to the Golden State Warriors on November 16, he also finished with ten points in addition to nine rebounds.

In a massive win over the Philadelphia 76ers on November 28, Pascal Siakam broke his career-high in points by going for 11 points in 24 minutes. He was four out of six from the field in that game. Then, in the final game of what was a six-game winning streak for the Toronto Raptors, Siakam went for a new career-high of 14 points on seven out of 12 shooting from the field in that 44-point win against the Atlanta Hawks.

After such a decent start early in the season for Pascal Siakam, he suddenly found himself seeing fewer minutes and touches on the floor. His role gradually decreased even though he still held on to his starting spot. Nevertheless, he went on to have respectable performances. One notable game that he had was on December 18. In that blowout win over the Orlando Magic, he had six points, seven rebounds, and a career-high four blocks. Then, on January 1, 2017, he went on to finish a win over the Los Angeles Lakers with ten rebounds and four blocks. After that, it went downhill for Siakam momentarily.

Pascal Siakam was surprised to know that he was going to lose his starting power forward spot to Lucas Nogueira. Despite not getting the same minutes that other starters had, Siakam held on to his starting spot and his role as an energy guy with passion and commitment. Siakam did not know why he was demoted to a bench spot and why he had lost his starting spot to someone who was not as versatile as he is. It caught him off guard that he suddenly was given a bench role.

What was worse than getting demoted to the bench was that Pascal Siakam's minutes also started to decrease. On January 5, his first game off the bench after starting the Toronto Raptors' first 34 games, he only played four minutes. He did not even see action in the next three games after getting demoted. When he did play a game, he only played about ten minutes with limited touches. It seemed as if he was merely there to fill in a spot on the floor while the other starters were resting.

After starting and playing all of the Raptors' first 34 games, Pascal Siakam saw himself missing six games in the month of January alone. He was healthy, and there was nothing wrong with his attitude. It was just that his coaches thought that they needed to give more minutes to the more established players on the roster instead of handing the starting spot to a raw and unproven rookie. Still, Pascal Siakam wanted to play.

Pascal Siakam rode the bench ever since he lost his starting job. He only saw minutes whenever the game was already out of hand or whenever someone got injured. Then, when the Toronto Raptors acquired big man Serge Ibaka, an African hero whom Siakam looked up when he was trying to get to the United States, he eventually saw himself seeing garbage time. Often, he did not even see a single minute at all because the Raptors already had enough veteran big men on the frontcourt.

For Pascal Siakam, he felt like it was unfair for him to be in such a predicament, especially because he worked hard to get there. At one point, he even questioned whether or not he belonged to the NBA. His rookie year was his very first exposure to the NBA experience. It was only then and there when he realized that the league was so full of great players, who themselves were working hard for their roster spots and minutes. Siakam saw and played against the best players in the world. He even wondered to himself if he indeed was someone who belonged in such a competitive league. He often asked whether he was not as great as any of the other guys in the NBA.[iv]

Then again, Siakam understood that he was not always going to get his way. He was sad deep inside, but he did not let that affect his team's chemistry or the way he approached his game. He knew that he was in the NBA for a reason and such a reason was not to merely fill a roster spot or to provide spot minutes for a starter for the rest of his NBA career.

Knowing that their rookie needed to hone his skills and seeing that Siakam just wanted to play basketball competitively, the Toronto Raptors sent him down to the NBA G-League (which was the D-League at that time). He played for the Raptors 905 in the G-League and went on to play their final five regular-season games. In those five games, Siakam released all his pent-up energy and averaged 18.2 points, 8.6 rebounds,

2.2 steals, and 1.6 blocks against players that had the talent to make it to the NBA.

Pascal Siakam powered the Raptors 905 to the NBA G-League Finals, where he got his first taste of success as a basketball player. He led his team to the G-League championship and was named the Finals MVP. Siakam averaged 23 points and nine rebounds in the three G-League Finals games that he played. As small an accomplishment as it was compared to that of other NBA players, Pascal Siakam understood that being in the G-League and winning the title and the Finals MVP was a part of his development as a man and a basketball player.

Pascal Siakam returned to the Toronto Raptors' active roster on May 1 just in time for the start of the second round of the playoffs. However, he only saw a total of ten minutes in that series against the Cleveland Cavaliers as the Toronto Raptors ended up getting swept in four games.

Throughout that season, Pascal Siakam averaged 4.2 points and 3.4 rebounds in the 55 games he played for the Toronto Raptors. He averaged 15.6 minutes a night and was showing flashes of his versatility on both ends. However, being a versatile role player was not enough for him. Siakam knew for a fact that he needed to become a better basketball player overall if he wanted to stay in the roster and contribute to the Raptors' success.

Playing with the Bench Mob

After a disappointing yet still successful rookie year for Pascal Siakam, the NBA's reigning G-League Finals MVP put in the necessary work to improve his game. He did so right after the Toronto Raptors got swept out of the playoffs. After spending a bit of time in the Dominican Republic for a short vacation, he went to Los Angeles to work alongside some of his teammates. He recounted that he only took a single day off ever since he started his offseason training.[iv]

Pascal Siakam knew what he needed to work on during the offseason after his coaches gave him a list of things he must improve on. They told him that he needed to become a better ball-handler and a more consistent jump shooter. To that end, he started working on the foundational skills that eventually helped him transform into the versatile player he is today.

During the offseason, Pascal Siakam improved his outside shooting by shooting 100 three-pointers from each corner and elbow. Then, he shot 50 more three-pointers from seven different spots on the floor while he was moving. At times, he doubled his effort and made over a thousand three-pointers in a single day. Siakam always had a good shooting form. He never had many problems with his mechanics. All he needed was to become a more consistent outside shooter and to gain the confidence he needed to become an effective player shooting from that distance.

Then, when it came to ball-handling, Pascal Siakam had a different approach to his improving that part of his game. The 6'9" power forward played the point guard position during scrimmages with his fellow NBA players.[iv] This was not an entirely new role for him. After all, back in college, he sometimes played as an isolation ball-handler from the elbow. While he was not a good ball-handler, he could handle the rock well enough for him to be able to drive to the basket.

The NBA is an entirely different beast. Pascal Siakam needed to remember that he could handle the ball. He needed to gain his confidence back instead of trying to fit in with his role as a mere energy guy playing spot minutes. To do that, he needed to improve his handlers and to become a point forward. Playing the point guard position during the offseason when scrimmaging against other NBA players helped him hone his talents as a ball-handling big man. If not, it made him more confident in his ability to carry the ball both in transition and in half-court sets.

When the 2017-18 season started, Pascal Siakam barely saw action. On October 19, 2017, he only was not able to score a single point and played only five minutes. Then, in his second game, he had eight minutes and finished with four points and six rebounds. In the Toronto Raptors' third game that season, he did not even play a single minute.

After barely playing in the first three games of the season, Pascal Siakam thought that maybe all the hard work he put himself through during the offseason had been put to waste. He was unable to impress his coaches and was stuck on the bench playing spot minutes. Siakam was asking himself whether or not all the training he had during the offseason even worked at all. Was he going to be stuck on the bench his entire career?

Pascal Siakam's luck turned around on October 25. Starting center Jonas Valanciunas was unavailable because of an injury. This led Dwane Casey to give the starting spot to Siakam even for just a single game. Knowing that this was his time to shine and that nobody was going to take that moment away from him, the Cameroonian big man played his best NBA game at that point in his career.[iv]

Against the Golden State Warriors, who were the NBA's defending champions that season, he played out of his mind and was one of the reasons the Toronto Raptors were competitive in that game. He made two three-pointers, which were the first three-pointers he has ever made in his entire career. Pascal Siakam also finished that game with a career-high 20 points after making nine of his 12 shots.

After that performance, Pascal Siakam earned the respect of his coaching staff. Two days after playing the Warriors, he started for the Raptors once again and went for 18 points on eight out of ten shooting from the floor in a win over the Los Angeles Lakers. Siakam did not regain the starting spot he had when he was a rookie, but he did earn more minutes from that point forward. He became one of the best players on the Toronto Raptors' bench, which was arguably the top bench in the entire league at that time.

Earning another starting spot for at least one more game, Pascal Siakam had one of the best all-around performances of his young career on November 17 against the New York Knicks. In that win, he played 34 minutes and went on to register 13 points, four rebounds, three blocks, and a career-high of five assists. That one game was but a mere showcase of what Siakam was able to do in the future as a terrific all-around player for the Toronto Raptors. On November 25, he had another similar performance in a 34-point win over the Atlanta Hawks. Siakam played 31 minutes off the bench and finished with 13 points, four rebounds, four assists, two steals, and one block.

On December 20, playing about 18 minutes off the bench, Pascal Siakam went on to have 14 points, six rebounds, four assists, and a steal in a blowout win over the Charlotte Hornets. After that game, it took a while for Pascal Siakam to break into double digits once again. Nevertheless, he was a sparkplug off the bench for the Toronto Raptors, who were holding on to their spot as the top team in the Eastern Conference. Even if he was not scoring well or making his three-pointers (there was a point wherein he missed 27 consecutive three-pointers), Siakam was a positive jolt of energy for the Toronto Raptors, who were playing better when he was on the floor.

Pascal Siakam broke his scoring slump on January 11, 2018. In 23 minutes off the bench, the rising Cameroonian big man finished with 16 points, eight rebounds, and four assists in a 34-point win over the Cleveland Cavaliers. Siakam improved so strategy that season that he was getting respect from defenses, who had to plan their defense with the Cameroonian in mind even though he was playing off the bench. While some thought that bench players Fred VanVleet, Delon

Wright, and CJ Miles were the best players off the bench for the Toronto Raptors, Pascal Siakam was their most versatile bench player because of what he could do on both ends of the floor.

Snubbed as a participant for the 2018 Rising Stars Challenge, the Cameroonian power forward had a pretty memorable month of February. That month was his most productive one as a scorer because that was when he put up the highest number of double-digit scoring games he had in a calendar month that season. In February, he had a total of seven double-digit scoring games in the 11 games that he played. His highest scoring performances were a pair of back-to-back 17-point games. That month, Pascal Siakam averaged 11 points on 62.2% shooting from the field.

However, Pascal Siakam was not only a much-improved scorer that season but had already grown into a capable ball-handler and passer to the point that his teammates learned to trust his decision-making.

Siakam realized this when he noticed that his teammates would rather run hard in transition whenever he a defensive rebound rather than asking the ball from him. He confirmed this from point guard Kyle Lowry when the All-Star playmaker told him to push the ball in transition after grabbing a defensive rebound instead of wasting time finding other ball-handlers.[iv] The reason was that everyone on the roster trusted his ability to handle the ball in transition and to make plays for others on the break. Lowry told him that they were always going to run in transition and were not going to go back to get the ball from him.

At the end of the regular season, Pascal Siakam averaged improved numbers of 7.3 points, 4.5 rebounds, and two assists. He improved his field goal percentage to 50.8% and had a positive net rating for the Toronto Raptors whenever he was on the floor. His defensive plus/minus was what made the difference as the Raptors were seemingly better when he was out on the floor.

The numbers might not show much of an improvement, but looking at them deeper showed how much Siakam grew in a span of only one season. After making a single three-pointer out of the seven he attempted during his rookie year, he made a total of 29 in his second year. After collecting a total of only 17 assists when he was a rookie, he had a total of 159 assists in that season. His coaches back in New Mexico were right when they said that Siakam was a speedy study.

More importantly, Pascal Siakam was a major contributor to the Toronto Raptors' season. He was arguably their best player because of his versatility and two-way abilities. The Raptors' "Bench Mob" was among the best in the entire NBA and was one of the best reasons why Toronto ended up winning 59 regular-season games to earn the top seed in the Eastern Conference heading into the playoffs.

Failing to score a single playoff point a year ago, Pascal Siakam scored his first playoff points after making a corner three-pointer in Game 1 of their first-round series against the Washington Wizards. He finished that game with a total of nine points alongside five rebounds as the Toronto Raptors drew first blood. Toronto eventually took a 2-0 lead but eventually got into a 2-2 deadlock with the Wizards heading into Game 5.

After the Toronto Raptors won Game 5, Pascal Siakam contributed in a big way in Game 6 to seal the series win in favor of his team. In the 22 minutes he played in Game 6, Siakam finished with 11 points and eight rebounds after making five of his six shots and collecting three offensive boards. He averaged 6.3 points on 56% shooting from the field in that series against the Washington Wizards.

While Pascal Siakam had 11 points on a terrific four out of five shooting clip from the field in Game 1 against the Cleveland Cavaliers in the second round, nothing right happened for the Raptors. LeBron James and his Cavaliers still had their numbers in the playoffs as the Raptors were once again swept out of the postseason at the hands of their long-time tormentors. The loss to the Cavs put the Raptors back to square one as they needed to make changes.

Nevertheless, what the entire organization was hopeful of was that they had a gem in Pascal Siakam. Everyone on the roster loved what he could bring on the floor. He showed plenty of versatility on both ends of the court because of his ability to hit outside shots, carry the ball in transition, make plays for teammates, and defend all five positions. Because of his versatility, many were beginning to compare him to Draymond Green. If he kept improving just as much as he did, the sky was the limit for both him and the Toronto Raptors.

Breakout Season, First NBA Championship, Winning the Most Improved Player Award

During the offseason, the Toronto Raptors surprised the entire world by breaking their core duo of All-Stars apart. They traded DeMar DeRozan to acquire superstar small forward Kawhi Leonard from the San Antonio Spurs. On top of that, they also replaced former head coach Dwane Casey with former assistant coach Nick Nurse. There might have been drastic changes, but the Toronto Raptors kept their core role players. Everyone believed that the key to that core was Pascal Siakam.

To that end, Pascal Siakam continued to work hard on his game during the offseason of 2018. He went back to Los Angeles and played scrimmages with fellow NBA players. The coaches who helped him train during the offseason were all impressed by how far Siakam had improved in a single summer. He grew into a much better athletic specimen and could showcase his ability to run the floor hard in transition either as the first the finisher or as the ball-handler. The best part was that he was never unselfish whenever he had the ball in his hands. This led to people believing that he was indeed a Draymond Green type of a player.

Rico Hines, who was in charge of the daily workouts that Siakam and the other Raptors players had to do during the summer, had plenty of praise to give the rising Cameroonian. Already impressed with Siakam's ability to push the ball in transition just as quick as any other guard and his defensive versatility, what Hines loved about the incoming third-year player was his work ethic. He has had the opportunity to work with many NBA players in the past, but Rico Hines believed that Pascal Siakam was the hardest working player with whom he has ever worked.[vii]

Rico Hines was not the only person who loved what Pascal Siakam brought to the floor. All the other stars who worked with Hines that summer praised the Cameroonian's improvement. Hines said that Siakam got the greatest number of praises out of anybody else that summer because of his amazing growth as a rising player. All-Stars Chris Paul and James Harden had nothing but positive praises for the young Raptor, who was poised to have a breakout season.[vii] However, despite how much he improved during the summer, nobody expected him to be able to rise as quickly as he did during the 2018-19 season.

When the 2018-19 regular began, new head coach Nick Nurse decided to start Pascal Siakam at the power forward position and opted to put Serge Ibaka at the center spot while playing former starting center Jonas Valanciunas off the bench. Having a frontline of Siakam and Ibaka gave the Raptors a more mobile lineup. They also provided plenty of floor spacing and defensive versatility to give new star player Kawhi Leonard enough space to operate.

Pascal Siakam made his season debut on October 17, 2018, against the Cleveland Cavaliers. Playing only 20 minutes that night, he finished with 13 points but made six of his eight shots. Three days later, he had his first double-double of the season after finishing a win over the Washington Wizards with ten points and ten rebounds. While he started the season a bit slow, he eventually found his groove as the Raptors' campaign progressed and as everyone adjusted to Nurse's new style and Kawhi Leonard's brand of basketball.

On October 29, Pascal Siakam had his breakout game after finishing with a career-high of 22 points alongside eight rebounds and four steals in a loss to the Milwaukee Bucks. A night later, he went for a dominant output of 15 points and three steals alongside a new career-high of 15 rebounds in a win over the Philadelphia 76ers. From then on, Pascal Siakam continued to rise.

Against LeBron James' Los Angeles Lakers on November 4, Pascal Siakam posted another double-double output. He finished that win with 16 points and 13 rebounds. After that, he continued a scoring tear that saw him scoring in double digits in 14 consecutive games. In those 14 games, he scored 20 or more points at five times. This included a new career-high of 23 points in a win over the New York Knicks on November 10. During that fantastic personal run, Siakam averaged 17 points on an amazing 63.8% shooting clip from the floor. At that point, he was proving himself as a rising star for the Toronto Raptors, who also learned to rely more on their young Cameroonian power forward.

On November 29 in a win over the two-time defending champions, Pascal Siakam proved himself a matchup nightmare for the Golden State Warriors. He had his best game at that point of the season after making eight of his ten shots and shooting three out of four from the three-point area to finish the game with a new career-best of 26 points. He was no longer a Draymond Green type of a player but had grown into a much more versatile offensive force in his third year in the NBA.

Pascal Siakam started the year 2019 well. On January 1, 2019, began what eventually became a momentous 2019 by going for a new career-high of 28 points to go along with ten rebounds in a win over the Utah Jazz. Then, just four days later, he recorded a new career-high in points by going for 30 points on 11 out of 15 shooting from the field in a win over the Milwaukee Bucks.

Proving that he was not merely an improved scorer, Pascal Siakam went for a new career-high of 19 rebounds in a win over the Washington Wizards on January 13. He also added 24 points, three steals, and two blocks in that all-around performance. Proving his mastery over the Washington Wizards' defense, Siakam went for a new career-high of 44 points and ten rebounds in a win on February 13. He made 15 of his 25 shots and four of his five three-pointers in that win. This career breakout game came just six days after he had 33 points and 14 rebounds in a win over the Atlanta Hawks. Siakam also became one of only

11 players in franchise history to score 40 or more points in a single game.

After that performance, there was no denying the fact that Pascal Siakam was no longer a secret. He was quickly becoming the Toronto Raptors' second-best player after Kawhi Leonard and was arguably just as critical to the team's success as All-Star point guard Kyle Lowry, who himself learned to defer to the rising Cameroonian when it came to scoring. Even when the Raptors acquired former All-Star center Marc Gasol in a trade, Siakam was still a major factor on both ends of the floor. As such, Siakam was staking his claim to the Most Improved Player award at that point of the season.

The Toronto Raptors indeed made several off-season and mid-season changes. They acquired Kawhi Leonard and made him the team's premier player. Danny Green, who was a part of that Leonard trade, was also doing well as the starting shooting guard.

Meanwhile, Marc Gasol proved to be the same defensive force he always has been. Even Kyle Lowry, who became more of a facilitator than a scorer, also made significant changes to the way he played that season.

However, despite all those changes and adjustments, it was hard to argue against the possibility that Pascal Siakam was the X-factor for the Toronto Raptors' success that season. You could say that Kawhi Leonard and Kyle Lowry were their most critical players. Both Marc Gasol and Serge Ibaka also provided plenty of defensive toughness for the Toronto Raptors. However, Siakam's rise as a surprising all-around option on both ends of the floor for the Raptors caught everyone in the league off guard.

When Pascal Siakam was hot, there was almost no way to defend the Toronto Raptors. Planning a defense centered around Leonard's great offensive capabilities and Lowry's shooting and scoring were already difficult enough, but what made the Raptors so difficult to defend was Siakam's rise. If teams put more emphasis on defending Leonard and Lowry, Siakam took control. If they planned their defense to stop Siakam, the Raptors' All-Star duo would have an easier time on the offensive end. Not many will give Pascal Siakam the credit he deserved that season, but there was no doubt that he was becoming one of the most crucial players on the roster.

The season progressed, and Pascal Siakam was only getting better and better. He had 33 points, 13 rebounds, and six assists in a win over the Oklahoma City Thunder on March 20. Then, on March 28, he went for 31 points, five rebounds, and five assists in a win over the New York Knicks. When the season was nearing its end, Siakam went for 28 points, ten rebounds, and five assists over the Brooklyn Nets in a win.

At the end of the regular season, Pascal Siakam averaged improved numbers of 16.9 points, 6.9 rebounds, and 3.1 assists. He was second only to Kawhi Leonard in terms of scoring while also averaging insanely efficient shooting numbers of 55% from the floor and 37% from the three-point area. He was undeniably a better scorer, finisher, shooter, ball-handler, and playmaker that season. Because of his amazing and consistent play, the Toronto Raptors won 58 games that season and were able to finish with the second-best regular-season record heading into the playoffs.

However, Pascal Siakam's drastic improvement was not merely a product of Kawhi Leonard's superstar presence or of Kyle Lowry's ability to find open teammates. Regarded merely as a finisher off of his teammates' ability to break defenses down and to create open opportunities ever since he was in college, Siakam grew into a player that could create his own shots.

The previous season, 68.8% of Siakam's two-point field goals came from assists. However, that number dropped to 49.3% during the 2018-19 regular season as he had learned to create shot opportunities and was converting his baskets whenever he drove to the rim or posted his man down low. Instead of being someone waiting for passes or for offensive rebound opportunities to score baskets, Siakam became a more assertive scorer who finished his own transition baskets after securing a rebound. He also learned to become a more creative finisher and learned how to finish acrobatic layups, floaters, and strong inside scoring attempts against contact.

Siakam also mastered the art of the spin move, which allowed him to get to the basket when driving out from the three-point line. It was a move he often went to whenever his man could recover on him after he initially blows past him or whenever there is a help defender waiting at the basket. This spin move was what ultimately completed his driving game, which was often the subject of criticism by scouts back when he was in college since he was not always able to go close to the basket whenever he was driving. He credited his soccer background for his patented spin move.[viii]

More importantly, it was rare to see Pascal Siakam having an off night that season. Even when he was not able to create open shots for himself, he was always there in the middle of every play waiting for his shots or playing tough defense. He retained the same outlook he has always had on basketball and was still the very same player who played like he was trying to make an NBA roster. Siakam's motor, energy, and effort were always consistent factors for the Toronto Raptors that season as they could always rely on their rising Cameroonian power forward to play his hardest every single night. As what coach Nick Nurse said, the real guys will always be out there playing hard night in and night out.[ix] He was, of course, referring to Pascal Siakam.

When everyone thought that Pascal Siakam could not get any better anymore that season, he proved everyone wrong during the playoffs. He was big for the Toronto Raptors in the first round of the playoffs in their series against the Orlando Magic. While his team may have lost Game 1 even though he finished that one with 24 points, he continued to stay consistent throughout the remainder of the series. Pascal had 30 points, 11 rebounds, and four assists in Game 3. Then, in Game 5, he helped wrap the series up in five games by going for 24 points. In that five-game series against the Magic, Siakam averaged 22.6 points, 8.4 rebounds, and three assists while shooting 53.3% from the floor.

The second round was a tough one for the Toronto Raptors as they had to battle a defensive type of series against the Philadelphia 76ers for a total of seven games. While he had grown into a terrific offensive player at that point in his career, it was ability to play help defense that allowed the Raptors to contain superstar center Joel Embiid in that series. He even outplayed his fellow Cameroonian in the second round.

Marc Gasol was the primary defender tasked in keeping Embiid away from the paint. However, Pascal Siakam played great help defense on the superstar, who averaged more than 27 points during the regular season. Whenever Embiid was in a good position inside the paint, Siakam was always there helping either Gasol or Ibaka out to make things difficult for the Cameroonian center. Then when Embiid was out on the perimeter shooting jumpers, Siakam was also there contesting his outside shots.

Siakam not only outplayed his fellow Cameroonian on the defensive end but also the offensive end as well. In that series, Siakam scored 20 or more points five times while averaging 19.4 points and 6.4 rebounds in seven games. Meanwhile, he helped contain Joel Embiid to only 17.6 points on a 37% shooting clip in that seven-game series.

While it was Kawhi Leonard, who hit a miraculous jumper at the end of Game 7, who won the series for the Toronto Raptors, Siakam was their second-best player on both ends of the floor in that tough second-round matchup. He was an unsung hero that made things tougher for the Sixers' best players while also proving that he was a matchup nightmare for any of Philadelphia's big men. However, things only got tougher for him in the Eastern Conference Finals.

In the Toronto Raptors' Eastern Conference Finals matchup with the league-leading Milwaukee Bucks, Pascal Siakam had the unenviable task of being the primary defender on the dominant Greek-born African player Giannis Antetokounmpo, who was eventually crowned the NBA's MVP that season and was also the most unstoppable inside presence in the league because of his rare combination of length, mobility, strength, and athleticism. The only player that could match up well with such a player was Siakam, who is almost equally mobile, long, and athletic.

To start the series off, the Toronto Raptors fell into a 0-2 hole as they allowed Giannis to average 27 points and 15.5 rebounds in Games 1 and 2. However, in Game 3, Pascal Siakam showed up on both ends of the floor. He was still Antetokounmpo's primary defender but allowed himself to receive help from different teammates to try to give the league's most dominant player different types of looks. This also allowed Pascal Siakam to perform well on the offensive end. He finished Game 3 with 25 points and 11 rebounds as the Raptors escaped with a double-overtime win. Meanwhile, Antetokounmpo was limited to 12 points on five out of 16 from the floor.

From then on, Siakam continued to make life difficult for the eventual MVP. One of Giannis' main weapons was his ability to drive past his defender out on the perimeter because of his long strides, quick first step, and ball-handling skills. However, Siakam could keep in step with him because of his great lateral movement and his ability to make contact. While Siakam was not a player strong enough to contain Antetokounmpo once the Greek Freak got too close to the basket, he slowed Giannis well enough to allow help defenders to contest his shots inside the paint.

After starting the first two games averaging 27 points, Giannis Antetokounmpo got limited to 20.5 points on 43.5% shooting from the field from Games 3 to 6. Pascal Siakam made life difficult for him as he was probably the only player in the league who was close to being a good physical matchup to the Greek Freak. Thanks to how Siakam's focus on defense could contain Antetokounmpo, the Toronto Raptors won Games 3 to 6 after losing the first two games. For the first time in franchise history, the Raptors were heading to the NBA Finals.

In that series against the Bucks, Pascal Siakam averaged 14.5 points and 6.5 rebounds. While Kawhi Leonard's offensive mastery was the highlight of that series once again, Siakam's defense was a major factor for helping them get to the Finals for the first time. For the second time during the playoffs, he was one of the players responsible for making life difficult for the opposing team's superstar. It is not an easy task to contain Joel Embiid and to make life difficult for Giannis Antetokounmpo. However, Pascal Siakam could do it.

Siakam's versatility was something that the Toronto Raptors needed in the NBA Finals. They were facing the Golden State Warriors, who were the heavy favorites to win that series even though they were missing Kevin Durant, who was arguably the best player in the NBA at that time. The Warriors were a different team compared to the Magic, Sixers, and Bucks because they did not have a dominant inside presence. Instead, they relied so much on their outside shooting and ball movement that opposing defenses needed a player who could switch out on the perimeter to guard shooters and ball-handlers. More importantly, the Raptors needed someone who could match

Draymond Green's energy on both ends of the floor. That someone was Pascal Siakam.

Branded as the Raptors' version of Draymond Green a season ago, Pascal Siakam had grown into a unique type of player. He was not only as versatile as Green is on the defensive end but had grown to become a more capable scorer. It was his ability to score well as a versatile offensive option that allowed the Toronto Raptors to surprise the entire world in Game 1 of the NBA Finals.

In Game 1 of the Finals, it was clear that the Golden State Warriors were hell-bent on stopping Kawhi Leonard, who was in the middle of one of the most impressive offensive performances in playoff history. However, they forgot about Pascal Siakam the entire game because their defenders were so focused on trying to stop Leonard from scoring.

Pascal Siakam took advantage of the looks he was given. The Warriors did not give him much attention inside or outside the paint. They left him out on the perimeter to shoot jumpers. When the Warriors' defenders were trying to stop Leonard's advances from the perimeter, Siakam was cutting and driving to the basket for easy layup or dunk opportunities or was feasting against defensive mismatches, especially when a guard switched out on him. In transition, the two-time defending champions did not have a big man that could match up with the streaking Pascal Siakam because Draymond Green was chasing guards and wingmen.

When the dust settled, the Toronto Raptors surprised the world after drawing first blood. However, what was more surprising was that Pascal Siakam led the way for the Raptors in that win. He finished Game 1 with 32 points, eight rebounds, and five assists while making 14 of his 17 shots from the field. He was also responsible for in crucial block on Draymond Green during a crucial point of the game. His versatile performance in Game 1 set the tempo up for the

Toronto Raptors as he forced the Golden State Warriors to rethink about their defensive strategy for the entire series. The defending champions had to come up with a game plan that could prevent Pascal Siakam from taking advantage of defensive mismatches and transition opportunities.

Whatever the Warriors did in Game 2 worked as Pascal Siakam had his worst game that series. However, the Cameroonian's versatility eventually became too much to handle for the Golden State Warriors, who also had to play without injured players Kevin Durant and Klay Thompson. With Draymond Green carrying more of an offensive load than a defensive one to try to make up for the loss of the Warriors' injured stars, Pascal Siakam could take advantage.

In the Games 3 and 4 victories in favor of the Toronto Raptors, Siakam ended up with 18 and 19 points respectively. Then, when the Raptors wrapped the series up in Game 6, the rising Cameroonian power forward finished with 26 points and ten rebounds while playing all but two minutes of that game. In that Finals series, he was the Raptors' second-best player after averaging solid all-around numbers of 19.8 points, 7.5 rebounds, and 3.7 assists.

What was more crucial than his production during that series was that he could help in forcing an upset over the defending champions. The Toronto Raptors won the series in six games and hoisted the NBA championship trophy for the first time in franchise history. Eight years since the day he joined Luc Mbah a Moute's basketball camp in 2011 to learn how to play the sport and seven years since the day he went to the United States to try to chase his late father's dream of having a son playing in the NBA, Pascal Siakam was an NBA champion and became the first Cameroonian-born NBA player to win a title.

Nobody expected him to win a title and to become a stellar contributor to a championship run back in 2016 when 26 teams passed him up in the NBA draft. However, in only three years, he grew into one of the most versatile big men in the NBA and could make use of his talents and skills to win a championship as one of the best players on the floor for the Toronto Raptors. Had Tchamo Siakam been able to see his son hoisting a championship trophy, he would have been prouder of what Pascal had accomplished in his life as a basketball star.

After winning the NBA championship, Pascal Siakam still had one more accolade to collect. In the NBA's annual awards show, the Cameroonian completed a momentous 2019 by capturing the 2018-19 Most Improved Player award. It was the best way to cap off what was such a memorable season for Pascal Siakam, who now has an NBA championship and a major individual award under his belt.

Life Without Kawhi Leonard, Becoming the Franchise Player

After the Toronto Raptors won the 2019 NBA championship, Kawhi Leonard became a free agent. Early in July of that year, he announced that he was going to leave the Toronto Raptors to go to home to California and to play for the Los Angeles Clippers. While the Raptors were thankful for Leonard for helping them win their first NBA title, they were left without an established superstar.

Without Kawhi Leonard, the Toronto Raptors were back to square one. The roster did not have many assets to build on as their core of Kyle Lowry, Serge Ibaka, and Marc Gasol were getting older. This means that they had to rebuild from what was left of that 2018-19 championship roster. Luckily, Pascal Siakam was a player they could hopefully build a contender around.

The Raptors' hopes of repeating as champions might have left when Kawhi Leonard went to Los Angeles, but they still had a new franchise player in the form of Pascal Siakam. Kyle Lowry was still the heart and soul of that team and a player capable of putting up All-Star numbers. However, he was already getting older, and no longer had the fresh legs he once had. The same could be said of Marc Gasol, who was already declining at that point in his career. That said, Siakam effectively became the new face of the franchise and the player the Raptors could use as the centerpiece of their rebuilding efforts.

There are reasons to believe that Pascal Siakam was not going to be the type of talent that Kawhi Leonard is. However, the chances of him not becoming a future All-Star are slim because of how he works hard during the offseason. The franchise can bank on him, improving even more next season and that his numbers saw an increase because of how he was going to get more touches. However, there is also a reason to believe that he will not be as efficient as he was during the 2018-19 season because defenses will be more focused on keeping him away from his spots.

Regardless of what was going to happen to his stats and his production, Pascal Siakam being the new face of the franchise gave the Toronto Raptors many options. They could trade everyone and hopefully build around younger and fresher talents, or they could try to play the same way as they did during the 2018-19 season but with Siakam as their main guy instead of Leonard.

Whatever the Raptors were going to do, what was clear was that Pascal Siakam entered a new chapter of his life. He had proven himself a capable player playing behind a superstar. He already won an NBA title but as a secondary or even as a tertiary player. Now, he has a chance to prove that he can be a top guy in the NBA and that he could help make a team successful. That was Siakam's next test in life. The Raptors can only hope that he is up to the task.

Chapter 5: Personal Life

Pascal Siakam was born and raised in Cameroon. He lived in the big city of Douala until the age of 11. When he turned 11, he was sent to a seminary in Bafia, where he was raised to become a Catholic priest in St. Andrew's Seminary. He hardly saw his family from then on because he only got to go home to Douala during the summer breaks.

Before he got his big break as a basketball player, Pascal Siakam was the one groomed by his family to become a priest. He grew up a devout Catholic but did not want to become a priest. Instead, he wanted to play soccer professionally or to become a businessman or a public servant working alongside his father Tchamo, who served as a mayor of a small town in Cameroon.

Pascal Siakam was born the youngest of six siblings. His three older brothers picked up basketball at ages earlier than he did and eventually earned scholarships to play Division I basketball in the United States. Boris played at Western Kentucky, Christian attended IUPUI, while James went to Vanderbilt. Meanwhile, his two older sisters also left home to pursue their careers. Vanessa played professionally as a soccer player in South Africa. On the other hand, Raissa went to Washington to pursue a career in nursing.[x]

When Pascal Siakam was attending New Mexico and was about to start his season as a redshirt freshman in October of 2014, his father Tchamo Siakam died due to the internal injuries he sustained in a car crash in Cameroon. However, because he was waiting for the issuance of his US Visa and was running the risk of losing his scholarship, he did not go home to Cameroon to attend his father's funeral. Pascal would have wanted to, but his family and his coaches urged him to stay in the United States to pursue his NBA dream because that was what Tchamo would have wanted him to do.[i]

Chapter 6: Impact on Basketball

Pascal Siakam's unlikely and inspiring journey to the NBA and an NBA championship is his impact to basketball because it is the kind of story you rarely hear even in a league full of inspiring stories of players coming from nothing to become stars in the NBA. It is one of the best underdog stories in the history of the league.

Born and raised in Cameroon, Pascal Siakam did not have basketball in his radar even though he came from an athletic family with a father that wanted one of his sons to get to the NBA. Soccer was his sport at an early age, but he had to give up his dream of becoming a soccer player when his father told him that he was going to become a Catholic priest to embody his family's faith.

As devout a Catholic as he was in his early childhood days, he never wanted to be a priest. Pascal Siakam dreaded his life in the seminary and never truly loved the many years he stayed there. If it had not been the wish of his father, whom he respected and admired greatly, that he become a priest, Pascal Siakam would have never agreed to go to Bafia to study there. He eventually left the seminary for good when he graduated from St. Andrew's in 2012.

It was only by sheer luck that Pascal Siakam could live an entirely new life. During a summer break in 2011, he attended a basketball camp organized by Luc Mbah a Moute. The reason was that he wanted to do something fun with his friends before he went back to Bafia on a long bus ride to resume his studies and his training. He was only 15 years old when he picked up basketball.

A year later, he was barely 17 when he was chosen to take part in the Africa leg of Basketball Without Borders camp held in South Africa. Knowing that it was his ticket out of a life he never wanted, Pascal Siakam went to the camp. He impressed American scouts with his height, mobility, and athleticism. However, what made Siakam stand out was his drive and his effort. He was always in the middle of every play and was making a difference both on offense and defense. He did not have many basketball skills and was displaying raw fundamentals. However, coaches knew that nobody can ever teach a player the heart and passion which Siakam played.

In 2012, Pascal Siakam went to the United States, where he was eventually recruited by New Mexico because of his innate hustle and energy. Being in New Mexico was also a struggle for Siakam because he was not physically ready to play against bigger and stronger college basketball players. However, he spent a year honing his body and preparing himself for the rigors of the sport. Siakam eventually turned to become a college star after winning the WAC Freshman of the Year award in 2015 and the WAC Player of the Year award in 2016.

However, Pascal Siakam entered the 2016 NBA draft not knowing whether or not he was going to get drafted or if any team was interested in him. After all, he was still a raw and unproven prospect that did not have many basketball skills. All that he brought to the table were his innate effort and drive to become better. That was all the Raptors needed to see from him when they took him late in the first round.

Siakam did not have a good start to his NBA career even though he was given the starting power forward spot in his first 34 games. He eventually became a benchwarmer and G-League player as the season went on. He even began questioning whether or not he belonged in the NBA. However, that did not stop him from working hard.

Through his sheer drive to succeed and to become a better player, Pascal Siakam went on to become arguably the Raptors' best bench player during the 2017-18 season. By completing the set of skills that allowed him to become a versatile two-way threat for Toronto, he became a much-improved starting power forward in his third year in the league.

Putting up good numbers and showing off skills and abilities nobody thought he had when he first entered the NBA, Pascal Siakam was one of the most surprising stories during the 2018-19 season. He went on to become the Most Improved Player as well as an NBA champion that season. All that was thanks to how hard he worked on his skills even though he only started playing basketball seriously in 2012. It was also because he was willing to take risks.

The things that most people do not know about Siakam's story are the risks he had to take and the sacrifices he had to make. He did not know how to speak in English and knew nothing about the life in America when he took the gamble of going to the United States to pursue a dream that had no assurances for him as well. In 2014, he took the biggest risk in his life and sacrificed not being able to attend his father's funeral so that he could stay in the United States. Then in 2016, he took a gamble and tried for the NBA draft even though there was no assurance that a team was willing to give him a roster spot.

Seven years since the day he left Cameroon and never went back, Pascal Siakam was making life miserable for fellow Cameroonian Joel Embiid in the playoffs, was playing great one-on-one defense on 2019 MVP Giannis Antetokounmpo in the Conference Finals, and was outplaying Draymond Green in the NBA Finals on his way to his first NBA championship.

What does Pascal Siakam's story mean for all the younger basketball players out there who are yet to get their big break? It entails that hard work and determination are ultimately the deciding factor that will help you get to where you want to be and where you should be regardless of whether you are from a big city in America, a small and impoverished village in

Africa, a small town in the Philippines, or an unknown city in India. After all, hard work was what led Siakam to where he was destined to be. Had he not worked hard to get to the NBA, he might still be in Cameroon unsure right now unsure of what he wanted to do with his life.

Chapter 7: Legacy and Future

The biggest legacy that Pascal Siakam has already started to forge is that of hard work. He is one of the few players in the NBA that got to where he is by relying on drive and effort. A blue-collar worker by NBA standards, Siakam was never the most talented or the most skilled player, but he got by because of how much time he spent on honing his game and on materializing his innate motor and passion to succeed in his chosen endeavor.

Pascal Siakam and a few of the other hard workers in the NBA is a testament to the fact that talent and skill are not always what brings you to the dance. There are those who are on the dance floor because they worked hard to get there. They fought hard against adversity and struggles to be able to strut their stuff. Siakam, who never got by with talent or skill, is on his way to stardom because he took many risks and made plenty of sacrifices to be able to make it to the NBA's biggest dance floor.

Alongside other African-born players, Pascal Siakam is also one of Africa's standard-bearers in the NBA. He and fellow Cameroonian Joel Embiid are two of the best African-born NBA players and are still young enough to be able to carry Africa's flag in the NBA for at least about a decade. There are not many African-born NBA players, but Siakam has become not only one of the best players coming from the continent of Africa but has also proven himself to be one of the brightest rising stars in the league. His story is an inspirational one to many Africans who are also hoping to make it to the NBA.

As a Raptor, Pascal Siakam carries a franchise legacy that started with Vince Carter in the 90s, passed on to Chris Bosh in the 2000s, and was carried by DeMar DeRozan during the most recent decade. He is now effectively the Raptors' franchise player considering that Kawhi Leonard spent only a year with the team. While he is yet to become the star players that Carter, Bosh, and DeRozan were in their time in Toronto, he could do something they were not able to do when they were Raptors—winning a championship.

That said, Pascal Siakam still has a long way to go before we could truly say that he has made his mark on the NBA and the Toronto Raptors. He may have to prove himself as an All-Star first and as someone who could carry a franchise before we could put him on the map. Nevertheless, he has always been a hard worker and someone who approaches the game as if his life depended on it. Those qualities should hopefully be enough for him to be able to forge a long-lasting career full of legacies and accomplishments.

Final Word/About the Author

I was born and raised in Norwalk, Connecticut. Growing up, I could often be found spending many nights watching basketball, soccer, and football matches with my father in the family living room. I love sports and everything that sports can embody. I believe that sports are one of most genuine forms of competition, heart, and determination. I write my works to learn more about influential athletes in the hopes that from my writing, you the reader can walk away inspired to put in an equal if not greater amount of hard work and perseverance to pursue your goals. If you enjoyed *Pascal Siakam: The Inspiring Story of One of Basketball's Rising Stars,* please leave a review! Also, you can read more of my works on *Roger Federer, Novak Djokovic, Andrew Luck, Rob Gronkowski, Brett Favre, Calvin Johnson, Drew Brees, J.J. Watt, Colin Kaepernick, Aaron Rodgers, Peyton Manning, Tom Brady, Russell Wilson, Michael Jordan, LeBron James, Kyrie Irving, Klay Thompson,*

Stephen Curry, Kevin Durant, Russell Westbrook, Anthony Davis, Chris Paul, Blake Griffin, Kobe Bryant, Joakim Noah, Scottie Pippen, Carmelo Anthony, Kevin Love, Grant Hill, Tracy McGrady, Vince Carter, Patrick Ewing, Karl Malone, Tony Parker, Allen Iverson, Hakeem Olajuwon, Reggie Miller, Michael Carter-Williams, John Wall, James Harden, Tim Duncan, Steve Nash, Draymond Green, Kawhi Leonard, Dwyane Wade, Ray Allen, Pau Gasol, Dirk Nowitzki, Jimmy Butler, Paul Pierce, Manu Ginobili, Pete Maravich, Larry Bird, Kyle Lowry, Jason Kidd, David Robinson, LaMarcus Aldridge, Derrick Rose, Paul George, Kevin Garnett, Chris Paul, Marc Gasol, Yao Ming, Al Horford, Amar'e Stoudemire, DeMar DeRozan, Isaiah Thomas, Kemba Walker and Chris Bosh in the Kindle Store. If you love basketball, check out my website at claytongeoffreys.com to join my exclusive list where I let you know about my latest books and give you lots of goodies.

Like what you read? Please leave a review!

I write because I love sharing the stories of influential athletes like Pascal Siakam with fantastic readers like you. My readers inspire me to write more so please do not hesitate to let me know what you thought by leaving a review! If you love books on life, basketball, or productivity, check out my website at claytongeoffreys.com to join my exclusive list where I let you know about my latest books. Aside from being the first to hear about my latest releases, you can also download a free copy of *33 Life Lessons: Success Principles, Career Advice & Habits of Successful People*. See you there!

Clayton

References

[i]MacMullan, Jackie. "Inside Pascal Siakam's 6,000-mile journey to Raptors stardom". *ESPN*. 5 December 2018. Web.

[ii]Peters, Damien. "The unreal story of how Pascal Siakam became an NBA player". *Open Court*. 28 February 2019. Web.

[iii]Siakam, Pascal. "Taking a chance on the unknown". *The Players' Tribune*. 11 December 2016. Web.

[iv]Zwelling, Arden. "He could be special". *Sportsnet*. Web.

[v]*Draft Express*. Web.

[vi]Moore, C.J. "2016 NBA draft prospects: breaking down the pro future of Pascal Siakam". *Bleacher Report*. 24 June 2016. Web.

[vii]Zarum, Dave. "Siakam, Raptors' bench mob poised to build off summer success". *Sportsnet*. 11 September 2018. Web.

[viii] Armstrong, Laura. "Raptors star credits soccer for his patented spin move". *The Hamilton Spectator*. 6 December 2018. Web.

[ix]Rush, Curtis. "Toronto Raptors' Pascal Siakam no longer best-kept secret in NBA". *Forbes*. 1 March 2019. Web.

[x] Brady, Rachel. "Pascal Siakam's path to the NBA began with his father". *The Globe and Mail*. 11 November 2016. Web.

Manufactured by Amazon.ca
Bolton, ON

10599500R00072